HOW MANY LEGS?

Kes Gray and **Jim Field**

How many legs would there be

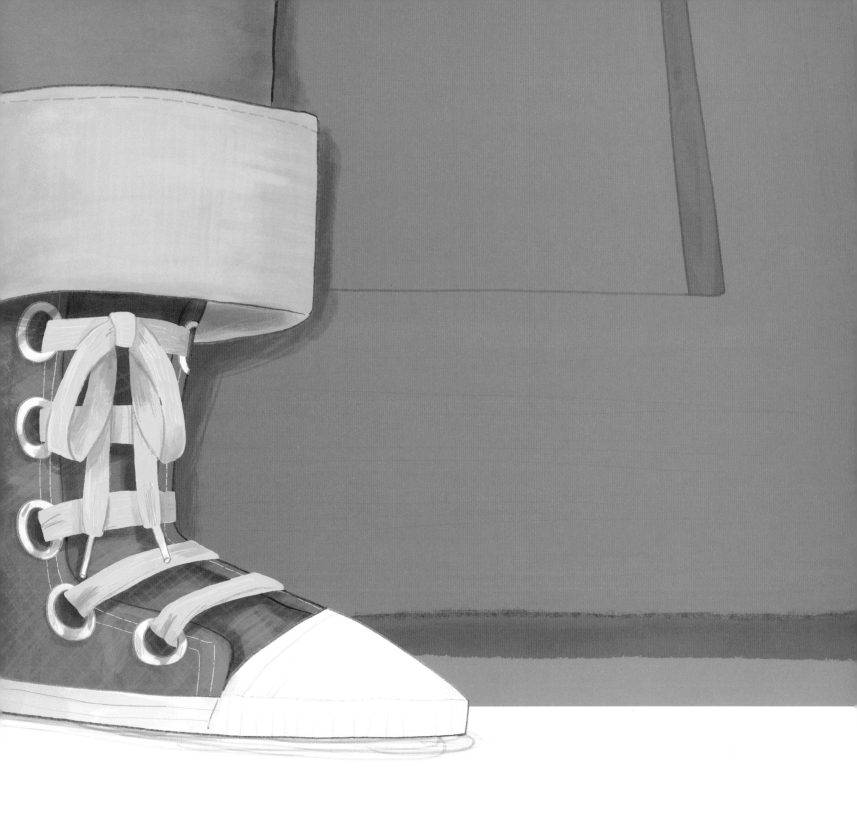

if in this room there was only me?

How many legs would there be
If a **polar bear** came for tea?

How many legs would it make
If a **duck** arrived with a lemon cake?

How many legs would be on view
If a **hippo** was invited too?

How many legs would you see if a **dog** walked in with a **chimpanzee?**

How many legs would be found
If a **seagull** joined us on the ground?

What would all
the legs come to
if a **frog** hopped in
on a **kangaroo?**

How high would the leg count go
If a **squid** rode in
on a **buffalo**?

How many legs would there be
If a **flea** flew in on a **bumble bee**?

Would the leg
count go right up
if an **octopus** and
a **pig** turned up?

Why would the number stay the same if a **slug**, a **snail** and a **maggot** came?

How would the number multiply
If a **centipede** came wiggling by?

How many legs would you find
If a **COW** walked in with a **goat** behind?

Leg-wise, what would be the score

if we were joined by a **dinosaur**?

2 + 4 + 2 + 4 +

10 + 4 + 6 + 6 +

+ 4 + 4 + 4 =

4 + 2 + 2 + 2 + 2 + 2 +

8 + 4 + 0 + 100

If you lose count don't feel bad,
A sum this big could send you mad.
No need to tie your brain in knots,
Let's just say the answer's...

The correct answer is...